HELLO,
ALEXANDER GRAHAM BELL

SPEAKING

A BIOGRAPHY

Taking part BOOKS

DP | DILLON PRESS, INC.
Minneapolis, Minnesota 55415

Cynthia Copeland Lewis

To Claire, my niece and favorite 10-year-old

Photographic Acknowledgments

The photographs are reproduced by permission of Alexander Graham Bell Collection, courtesy of the National Geographic Society (pages 27, 55, 58, 60, front and back cover); Alexander Graham Bell National Historic Site (pages 9, 11, 16, 18, 21, 37, 44); and by courtesy of AT&T Archives (pages 6, 24, 30, 32, 42, 49, 52).

Library of Congress Cataloging-in-Publication Data

Lewis, Cynthia Copeland, 1960-
     Hello, Alexander Graham Bell speaking : a biography / Cynthia Copeland Lewis.
         p. cm. — (Taking part books)
     Includes bibliographical references and index.
     Summary: A biography of the inventor of the telephone.
     ISBN 0-87518-486-3
     1. Bell, Alexander Graham, 1847-1922—Juvenile literature.
2. Inventors—United States—Biography—Juvenile literature.
[1. Bell, Alexander Graham, 1847-1922. 2. Inventors.] I. Title.
TK6143.B4L49 1991
621.385'092—dc20
[B]   91-7562
                                                                          CIP
                                                                          AC

Dillon Press, Inc., 242 Portland Avenue South
Minneapolis, Minnesota 55415

Printed in the United States of America
1 2 3 4 5 6 7 8 9 10 99 98 97 96 95 94 93 92 91

ABOUT THE AUTHOR

Cynthia Copeland Lewis is a free-lance writer and the author of several books for adults and young people. She has worked as a journalist, a children's magazine editor, and a corporate communications editor. Ms. Lewis is the founder of Book Buddies, a program that matches underprivileged children with sponsors who send one book a month to them.

The author has a degree in government from Smith College. She lives with her husband and two children in East Sullivan, New Hampshire.

Contents

ALEXANDER GRAHAM BELL

On a March day in 1876, Alexander Graham Bell sent a clear message over a telephone wire to Thomas Watson, his partner in a great scientific adventure. One line connected Bell to Watson during that famous experiment more than a century ago. Today there are many millions of telephone numbers, and the telephone is our most valuable means of communication.

Alexander Graham Bell III was born with talent, patience, and determination. His interests were shaped by the Bells of his native Scotland who came before him. As a young man, he used his father's invention, "Visible Speech," to teach deaf children how to speak. And his work with deaf children led him to explore new means of communication.

Fate brought him and his family to North America. In the city of Boston, he found the people and the resources necessary for the invention of the telephone. The telephone, and the Bell Telephone Company he helped to found, made him a millionaire. For the rest of his life, he worked on other inventions and improved at least one, Thomas Edison's phonograph. Bell gave generously to scientific projects, and especially to help deaf people such as his students and Helen Keller. Most people will remember Alexander Graham Bell as the inventor of the telephone. But first and foremost, he would have wanted to be remembered as a teacher of the deaf.

1

The Third Alexander

"Mr. Watson—Come here! I want to see you!"

Thomas Watson jumped from his chair. He had heard sounds come through the homemade telephone before, but never words so clear and distinct. He ran from the bedroom where the receiver was set up to the laboratory down the hall. There, his partner, Alexander Graham Bell, was sending the messages. When he told Bell that words had come over the wire, Bell asked Watson to repeat the sentence he had heard.

"You said, 'Mr. Watson, come here—I want to see you,'" Watson replied. Bell was delighted. The men changed places so that Bell could listen to Watson speak into the mouthpiece. Although they had waited many months to hear each other's voices this way, they had not prepared any speeches to deliver through

A portrait of Alexander Graham Bell holding his first telephone in his attic workshop in Boston.

the homemade telephone. Watson read from a book. Bell sang a song. Late into the night they took turns speaking and listening. Some words were clear, and others were not. That, however, was not important.

"This is a great day," Bell wrote in a letter to his father. "I feel that I have at last struck the solution of a great problem—and the day is coming when...friends will converse with each other without leaving home."

Could Bell have known on that March day in 1876 how important the telephone would become to people all over the world? Today it is our most valuable means of communication. In a matter of seconds, it links neighbor to neighbor, office to office, country to country. One line connected Bell and Watson during those famous experiments more than a hundred years ago. Could they have imagined that someday there would be millions of telephones in use around the world?

The first Alexander Bell was born on March 3,

This painting shows young Aleck Bell at the age of three.

1790. The second arrived on March 1, 1819.

The man the world would come to know as Alexander Graham Bell was born in Edinburgh, Scotland, on March 3, 1847. This third Alexander—called "Aleck" by his parents and brothers—shared more with his father and grandfather than their names. He shared their interests and ideas as well. His grandfather wrote books and gave lectures on speech impediments. A speech impediment is a problem such as stammering that makes it hard to understand someone. Aleck's father was a speech teacher who developed a special kind of alphabet called Visible Speech. This alphabet used pictures to show how the tongue and lips should move to make certain sounds. Deaf people and others who had trouble speaking learned how to talk using Visible Speech.

Aleck learned from his mother as well. She was deaf, but she taught all of her sons—Melville, Aleck, and Edward—at home when they were young. A talented painter and musician, Eliza Bell encouraged her children to play the piano. Only Aleck, though, seemed to have true musical talent. In fact, when he was a young boy, he dreamed of becoming a famous piano player.

Eliza Bell also taught her sons to believe in God and respect the Christian Sabbath, or Sunday. One Sunday, Aleck scolded his father for asking him to pose for a photograph. Young Aleck believed that Sunday was a day for prayer.

Even though he liked to spend time alone, reading or playing the piano, Aleck had lots of time for fun with his brothers and friends. One special friend was Ben Herdman, who was learning from Aleck's father how to correct his stammering. Often, he invited Aleck to play at his family's mill. It was just a short

In this early family photograph, Aleck (left) stands next to his brother Melville (back), his mother and father (front, center), and his brother Edward (right).

walk to Ben's house from Aleck's home in Edinburgh's busy, crowded Charlotte Square. But the mill was surrounded by fields and forest. To Aleck it seemed as if it were many miles from the city. The river's rushing water, the bridge, the pond, and the tall stone buildings with wonderful places for hide-and-seek made the mill a perfect place for boys to play.

Aleck's parents felt that such romping in the country was good for children. They often took their sons away from the city on hikes and other outings. Eventually, the Bells bought a country house where the family stayed at least two days a week. Aleck called this his real childhood home.

In the gardens at his country house, at the mill, and even in the city, Aleck found things he could collect. He began by collecting plants. But when his father urged him to label each plant with its proper Latin name, he lost interest in that project. Later he collected animals such as dogs, cats, mice, rabbits, and frogs. These he kept in pens and cages at the country house. Although Aleck was not cruel to these animals, he saw them as subjects of experiments, not as cuddly pets. He tried to teach his little black dog to speak by pressing on its throat, hoping to turn its growls into words.

Aleck collected more than live animals. When he and his friends found dead birds or toads in the yard, they saved them for experiments. Aleck and his friends liked to play a game in which they pretended to be teachers of different subjects. They held "classes" on the top floor of the Charlotte Square home where most of Aleck's collections were. Young "Professor Bell" was in charge of cutting open the dead animals. He showed the others where the various organs were located.

One day when he was teaching his "class," Aleck stuck a knife into a small, dead pig. Air that had been trapped inside the pig rushed from its body, making a noise like a moan. The startled "teacher" and his students scrambled to get out of the room. School was over for the day!

Even after this, Aleck was as interested in experimenting as ever. Ben's father thought that Aleck and Ben should do something useful around the mill rather than play all the time. He suggested that the boys find a way to take the husks off the small grains of wheat. Aleck took this task very seriously. After he tried different ways of cleaning the wheat and thought about what kinds of machines would be needed, he had an idea for Mr. Herdman. When the miller tried Aleck's wheat-husking device, he found that it worked.

Although he had a keen interest in these types of projects, young Aleck was not a top student. At the age of ten, he ended his home-schooling and entered Hamilton Place Academy. After a year there, he moved on to the Royal High School. Aleck enjoyed school sports such as gymnastics and cricket, but he hated his classes in Latin and Greek. Even though his math class was interesting at times, he was still bored by most of it. He only wanted to learn about things that excited him.

Perhaps because he did not perform well as a student, Aleck decided he wanted to set himself apart in some special way. The proud boy wanted his own name. He did not want to be the last in a line of "Alexander Bells." When a family friend named Alexander Graham visited from Canada, Aleck chose "Graham" for his new middle name.

March 3, 1858, was Aleck's eleventh birthday. At supper, the second Alexander raised his wine glass in a toast to the third Alexander. From that time on, young Aleck would be known as "Alexander Graham Bell."

2

Growing Up
and Good-byes

I am thirteen years old, I find;
Your birthday and mine are the same.
I want to inherit your mind,
As well as your much honored name.

Just two years after Aleck wrote that poem for his grandfather, he went to London to spend a year studying with the oldest Alexander.

Grandfather Bell's second wife had just died. He wanted to have his grandson near to keep him company. The older man also believed that he could help Aleck improve his grades. Because he wanted Aleck to act older and take his work more seriously, he bought his grandson proper clothes for a young man in London. Wearing his tall hat and gloves, and carrying a cane, Aleck must have felt many years and

Alexander Graham Bell about the time he lived in London with his grandfather.

Alexander Graham Bell, (left), his father (center), and his grandfather (right).

many miles away from his simple boyhood home on Charlotte Street.

In the elegant but dark and gloomy house at Harrington Square, Grandfather Bell taught Aleck how to speak correctly. In those days, it was important for young people to learn to use their voices in just the right way. Crowds came to hear famous men recite poems and plays, just as they flock to music concerts today. Day after day, the oldest Alexander and the youngest one read plays and speeches. Aleck practiced and practiced until he had them memorized. With so much attention from a man he respected, Aleck began to enjoy learning. He also liked getting an allowance and having the freedom to spend it as he wished.

As the year passed, Grandfather Bell became ill and needed Aleck's daily help. In this way, the young man began to learn responsibility, too. When his father came to get him at year's end, Aleck acted much more grown up and confident than when he had first come to London. He felt that this year had changed him from a boy into a man.

Before they left London, Aleck and his father stopped to visit a famous scientist named Sir Charles Wheatstone. Wheatstone showed the Bells one of his inventions called a "speaking machine." The device, which made sound like a human voice, delighted both father and son.

When the two returned home, Aleck's father challenged him and his older brother Melly to make a speaking machine of their own. He promised to give his sons a prize if they were successful.

First, the two boys studied a book Wheatstone had lent them. They decided that Melly should work on the lungs, throat, and larynx. The larynx is the part of the body that contains the vocal cords. To learn about how it worked, the brothers asked a butcher for a lamb's larynx to study. Aleck put together the head for the speaking machine. He made jaws, teeth, and a nasal cavity with a human skull as a model. Then he used rubber to make the lips and cheeks.

At last the time came to put the parts of the speaking machine together. Melly blew through the tube that acted like the throat while Aleck moved the lips and tongue. Out came a series of strange, high-pitched noises. The boys soon learned how to move the parts of the machine to make it wail, "Mama, mama, mama!" It sounded so much like a real infant crying that a woman from a nearby apartment rushed over to see what was wrong with the "baby." Their father was proud of the boys for working so long and hard on their invention. It pleased him that his sons now knew how human organs work to make sound.

Since he had returned from London, Aleck felt that his parents were treating him like a boy again.

Aleck Bell stands in front of a college in Scotland.

He thought of himself as a man. Aleck began thinking of ways to be on his own. For a while, he planned to hide on a ship and become a sailor. He decided instead to apply for a job as a student-teacher of music and speech.

During the fall and winter of 1863-1864, 16-year-old Alexander Graham Bell taught at Weston House on the northern coast of Scotland. In the summer that followed, he worked with his father on his Visible Speech. His father's work was gaining much attention in London. After a short time at the University of Edinburgh, Aleck returned to Weston House. While he was a teacher or a student, he worked on speech projects in his free time.

During the next five years, Aleck struggled with his parents as most young people do. He wanted more independence. Still, he also felt that he should do as his mother and father wished. When Aleck was 20 years old, his younger brother Edward, who had always been rather sickly, died of tuberculosis. In his diary, Aleck wrote, "Edward died this morning at ten minutes to 4 o'clock. He was only 18 years and 8 months old." This left his parents alone, because Aleck's older brother Melly had married and moved away. Aleck returned home to be with them.

He continued to teach, taking on his first deaf pupils a year later. The little girls, Lotty and Minna, were soon joined by Kate and Nelly, lovable eight-year-olds. Using Visible Speech, Aleck was able to teach them to say many words. Kate was excited about summer vacation when she could go home and show her parents what she had learned. She practiced saying, "I love you, Mama." Others soon learned of the young Bell's success and began asking him to teach their deaf children.

While Aleck was busy teaching his deaf students,

Melly and his wife, Carrie, were starting their family. They had a baby boy, Edward, in August 1868. Sadly, the baby was not healthy. In February 1870, he died. Melly, who had been ill, died three months later. The death of both brothers within two years upset Aleck greatly.

Aleck, too, had become thin and pale. His parents worried greatly that the only child they had left might become ill. His father begged him to move with them to Canada. Aleck wanted to stay in England, but he felt that he should do as his parents wished. And so, on July 21, 1870, Aleck, his parents, and Melly's widow prepared to sail for North America. Gathered at the train station to see them off were the old family nurse, a friend of Aleck's named Adam Scott, and the family dog.

On August 1, the Bells arrived in the Canadian province of Quebec.

3

Teacher Turns Inventor

The Bells paid $2,600 for a roomy house with a stable, a henhouse, an icehouse, and other buildings. Their new home was on a large plot of land outside Brantford, Ontario. The house sat high on a bluff overlooking a winding river. Here Aleck Bell would spend summer vacations and holidays for many years to come.

Young Bell, now 23, traveled to Boston, Massachusetts, to teach Visible Speech at schools in and around the city. He was amazed at all that Boston offered. The bustling New England city had the largest public library in the country and universities such as the Massachusetts Institute of Technology (MIT). Bell settled happily in his room on Beacon Hill and began teaching deaf pupils.

The Bell homestead at Tutelo Heights near Brantford, Ontario.

Soon, the young man from Scotland became well known for his work with the deaf. He dreamed of opening a teacher-training school to show others how to use Visible Speech to teach deaf students. From this time on, Alexander Graham Bell considered himself—before anything else—a teacher of the deaf.

One of his deaf pupils was 16-year-old Mabel Hubbard, a confident and intelligent young lady. She had become deaf 11 years earlier as a result of scarlet fever. When she first saw Bell, she did not like him. He was dressed carelessly and "seemed hardly a gentleman." But Bell's spirit and gentle manner soon changed her mind. She could not wait for her lessons with "Mr. Bell" and was flattered when he told her that her voice was "naturally sweet." Aleck had become quite fond of Mabel as well. Still, because she was deaf and ten years younger than he was, Bell did not tell anyone how he felt about her.

Another pupil was George Sanders, a five-year-

At the Pemberton Avenue School of the Deaf in Boston, Alexander Graham Bell (top of the stairs at right) trained the teachers to teach the deaf students.

old boy who had been born deaf. He enjoyed being with "Professor Bell" and liked to follow him, watching him do experiments. At first, the boy and his nurse lived in the boarding house with Bell. George's father wanted his son to spend as much time with Bell as he could. Later, Bell moved with George to his grandmother's house in Salem, a town near Boston.

Bell's interest in science was growing. In the fall of 1872, he began going to lectures at MIT and studying books about electricity at the library. In the 1870s, scientists and inventors all over the world were working on ways to improve communication. People contacted one another through mail or by telegraph. The telegraph sent messages by electricity. For each letter of the alphabet, there was a special code that was tapped out with a telegraph key. But in those days, only one message could be sent out over the wire at a time.

Bell became interested in an idea called the harmonic or multiple telegraph. With this device, a number of messages could be sent by Morse code on a single wire. Bell began to experiment in the evenings. During the day, he taught at Boston University and tutored his deaf students.

Night after night, Bell worked in his home

laboratory on his harmonic telegraph experiments. Many people, such as an inventor named Elisha Gray, were working on similar projects. Bell worried that another scientist would make a harmonic telegraph before he did. He worked such long hours that he often made himself ill.

It would take two years for him to do enough work on his idea to get a patent. When the government gives a patent to an inventor, he or she becomes the only one who can make, use, and sell the invention. Bell's harmonic telegraph was never used by the telegraph companies. But his work on that invention led him to develop his ideas for the telephone.

During the summer of 1874, Bell was 27 years old and vacationing in Brantford. He liked to relax at his "dreaming place" on the hill behind his parents' house. One July day, as he sat watching the river, he suddenly thought about sending voices over telegraph wires. Soon afterward, he asked his friend Clarence

J. Blake, a Boston ear doctor, for a human ear to use in his experiments.

For months Bell did not tell anyone about how he thought voices could travel many miles with lightning speed. He was afraid that people would think he was crazy. But later Aleck wrote his parents a letter describing his idea. He asked them to keep the note in case he needed to prove that he was the first one to have thought of the telephone.

In fall 1874, Bell made a deal with two men that would delay the invention of the telephone. George Sanders's father, Thomas, promised to give the young inventor the money he needed to work on his harmonic telegraph experiments. In return, he wanted Bell to share the patent rights with him. Gardiner Hubbard, Mabel's father, also became interested in Bell's work and made him a similar offer. In February

1875, the three men signed an official agreement. Their partnership was called the Bell Patent Association.

Bell needed the money from the two men. But now he had to put aside work on the telephone. Sanders and Hubbard did not want Bell to waste his time on the telephone. The businessmen were sure that the harmonic telegraph was a better idea. They never imagined that in time Bell's telephone would make them all rich.

In this portrait, Alexander Graham Bell and Thomas Watson examine the
first telephone in their attic workshop in 1875.

4

Birth of the Telephone

In another part of Boston, men were hard at work in Charles Williams's electrical shop. Thomas Watson was one of the shop's most creative and hardworking employees. This young man helped the inventors who came into the shop wanting special models made of their projects. And they helped him. Local inventors such as Thomas A. Edison, who later patented the phonograph, taught Watson many things about electricity.

In January 1875, Watson was assigned to work with Alexander Graham Bell. He remembered Bell as "a tall, slender...young man with a pale face, black side-whiskers and drooping mustache, big nose, and high, sloping forehead..." Bell worked with Watson on the harmonic telegraph that Sanders and Hubbard wanted. At last, the men produced a working model. In March, Bell traveled to Washington, D.C., to show it to the president of the Western Union Telegraph Company. This was the largest U.S. company, and the nation's only telegraph company.

While he was in Washington, Bell visited Joseph Henry. Henry was the director of the Smithsonian Institution and one of the country's leading scientists. Henry was so impressed with Bell's harmonic telegraph that Bell decided to tell the older man about his ideas for the telephone. Henry told the young inventor that he had "the germ of a great invention."

"What would you advise me to do: publish it and let others work it out or attempt to solve the problems myself?" Bell asked.

"You should perfect the invention yourself," Henry answered. Bell explained that he was not sure that he had the proper knowledge of electricity.

"Then get it!" Henry responded.

Excited, Bell returned to Boston. "I think that transmission of the human voice is much more nearly at hand than I had supposed," he wrote to his parents. But his business arrangement with Hubbard and Sanders meant that he had to finish working on the multiple telegraph first.

Day after day, night after night, he and Watson worked in the attic of the electrical shop. They strung a wire from one attic room to another. At one end was a transmitter, which worked like an ear. And at the other end was a receiver, or "mouth." With the transmitter, the men were able to turn sounds into a pattern of electric waves that traveled along the wire to the receiver. The receiver turned the pattern of electric waves back into sound. While Watson operated the transmitter, Bell sat nearly 60 feet away at the receiver, listening.

One steamy June day in 1875, as Watson was sending sound waves from the transmitter, a part of the device stuck. He plucked at it, trying to release it. In the other room, Bell waited. Suddenly, he saw the reed on the receiver move. This is what he had been waiting for. "What did you do?" Bell called out in an excited voice. "What did you do then? Don't change a thing! Let me see!"

Bell quieted all the machinery and told Watson to pluck at it again. His sensitive ear, trained for years in music, heard a faint, unfamiliar noise. It had a sound like a human voice! Bell later called this sound "undulatory" since it made noises that were high and low, loud and soft. Both men knew what an important discovery they had made. For the rest of the day and night, they repeated the experiment to make sure it had not been an accident. Time and time again, the results were the same.

Finally, Bell and Watson locked up the shop and said good-bye on the dark, deserted street. Bell was too excited to go home and sleep. He paced the city

Alexander Graham Bell in 1876, shortly after his first successful experiments with the telephone.

streets in the summer heat until it was almost dawn. Then he sat at his desk to write Hubbard a letter. It began, "I have accidentally made a discovery of the very greatest importance."

Nearly a month later, the men made another breakthrough. While Bell shouted into the latest version of the telephone from the attic, Watson listened below. Nothing happened. Bell sang. He whistled. But he heard no reply from Watson. Again he yelled. Suddenly Watson burst into the room.

"I could hear your voice plainly!" he exclaimed. "I could almost make out what you said!"

Now Bell was more convinced than ever that the telephone would be a success. He hoped to put all of his time and energy into the project. But Gardiner Hubbard insisted that Bell put the telephone work aside and work on the harmonic telegraph. Hubbard thought that the telephone was just a silly toy. Sadly, Bell agreed to continue with Hubbard's project.

Not until the next winter did he work on the telephone again. Bell applied for a patent on his use of an undulatory current of electricity. One of its uses, he wrote, was sending voices. Elisha Gray had been applying for similar patents. But Bell won. On March 3, 1876, his 29th birthday, the Patent Office approved his application for the basic telephone patent.

Alexander Graham Bell had been thinking of more than his successes with the telephone during the summer of 1875. He had fallen in love with his deaf student, Mabel Hubbard. In the midst of his experiments, he paused to write to her mother about his feelings. The Hubbards liked Alexander. But they felt that Mabel, just 17, was too young to consider marriage. Aleck's own parents were not sure that he and Mabel should be married. Because his mother was deaf, she worried that Aleck and Mabel might have deaf children.

After many talks with Mabel's parents, Alexander

convinced them that he would be a good husband for their daughter. On November 25, 1875, Thanksgiving Day as well as Mabel's 18th birthday, Mabel told Aleck that she loved him more than anyone—except her mother. They were engaged to be married. From then on, Thanksgiving Day held a special meaning for Alexander and Mabel. And from that day on, Aleck spelled his name without the *K* because Mabel liked it that way.

By early in the next year, Bell and Watson had moved the laboratory to several rooms in Exeter House, a boarding house. Just after the approval of the basic telephone patent, the partners tried the latest version of the telephone. This time, the sound of the voice made the wire move up and down in a dish of acid mixed with water. Bell waited while Watson set up the equipment in the other room. Suddenly he said, "Mr. Watson—come here! I want to see you!" Watson later wrote that Bell called him because he had spilled some burning acid on his clothes. Bell's laboratory notes, though, made no mention of this. In any case, the thrill of sending a clear voice over the wire made any injury to Bell seem unimportant.

At that time, only a handful of people knew how far Bell and Watson had come in their experiments. Bell decided to enter his telephone in the Centennial Exhibition in Philadelphia. There, it would be judged along with the exhibits of scientists from all over the world.

Sunday, June 25, 1876, dawned steamy and still. This was the day that Bell's exhibit and other sound exhibits were to be judged. While the judges stood listening to Elisha Gray talk about his inventions, the hot sun streamed in through the windows. Bell's turn came after Gray. But the sweaty judges looked ready to quit for the day. One of the judges, though, was Brazilian Emperor Dom Pedro, who had met Bell on a trip to Boston a few weeks earlier. The emperor

This is an artist's view of the historic moment at Philadelphia's Centennial Exposition of 1876, when Alexander Graham Bell demonstrated his new invention to Dom Pedro, emperor of Brazil.

insisted that the group visit Bell's exhibit. First, Bell explained his harmonic telegraph to the tired judges. Then he moved on to the telephone, explaining that he was still working on the invention. Bell went to the far end of the gallery. With Dom Pedro's ear pressed against the receiver, Bell began to recite from

Shakespeare's famous play, *Hamlet*: "To be or not to be..."

"A voice was speaking in my ear!" cried the startled emperor. One by one, the judges took turns listening. They were amazed at how clearly the words came over the wire! Even Gray was impressed. Alexander Graham Bell won the special Centennial Prize for both his harmonic telegraph and the telephone. And within a matter of weeks, people from around the globe had heard of Alexander Graham Bell and his incredible invention.

5

A Useless Toy?

The Centennial Prize made the telephone and its inventor famous. Still, most people thought of the telephone as a clever toy rather than something useful. Soon, the excitement over his victory in Philadelphia began to dim. Then some of his experiments to send speech over a long distance failed. Discouraged, the young inventor left Boston for his family home in Brantford in July 1876.

There he conducted three historic tests—tests that brought him and his telephone more attention. For his first test, Bell decided to send a message from the Brantford office of the telegraph company to a telephone in the nearby town of Mount Pleasant.

A crowd was beginning to gather in the Mount Pleasant general store as the time for the test neared.

After he had proved that his invention worked, Alexander Graham Bell had to demonstrate that the telephone was a useful instrument of communication.

Bell nervously looked at his watch. At the right time, he picked up the receiver. The crowd became silent. Bell listened. Then he heard the line that was used so often during those early telephone experiments: "To be or not to be..."

Everyone in Mount Pleasant wanted to hear, and everyone from Brantford wanted to speak. Alexander's Uncle David and other members of the family recited famous lines. This was the first successful one-way test of Bell's invention over a real telegraph wire. The final two tests were as successful as the first. But so far, the conversation had been one-sided.

Back in Boston, Watson had given up his work at the electrical shop to work full-time for Bell. Alexander paid him three dollars a day. He also gave him a share of the patent rights as well as free room and board at Exeter Place. In October, Bell firmly declared that all his time would now be spent on the telephone. The Brantford tests had convinced him—

and even Hubbard—that the harmonic telegraph was not important in and of itself. Rather, it was an early stage in the development of the telephone.

Bell and Watson decided to try to have the first long-distance, two-way conversation. They wanted to show how their telephone might be of use in business. In October 1876, they arranged to use a private telegraph line connecting a company's factory with its office, two miles away across the Charles River. Bell and Watson understood each other perfectly over the telegraph line. In fact, the voices had been clearer than in the laboratory. Bell called it "the proudest day of my life." The telephone worked!

There was still much work to be done. Bell compared his invention to a child who keeps growing and changing. The public finally began to respond. Letters piled up on Bell's desk with requests for telephones. But when the Bell Partnership tried to sell the invention to Western Union, President

William Orton said that he was not interested in Bell's electrical toy.

Bell needed money to get foreign patents for the telephone and to be able to marry Mabel. To make money quickly, he decided to demonstrate his invention before the public at lectures. The lectures were a huge success. In the years before the phonograph was widely available, people had never heard a voice coming from a mechanical device. It was like magic. One newspaper article about a telephone demonstration in the town of Salem featured the headline "Salem Witchcraft."

On April 4, 1877, newspapers announced that the world's first telephone line had been strung between Charles Williams's home in Somerville and his Boston shop. Alexander wrote eagerly to Mabel that now "the telephone is in practical use."

The Bell Telephone Company was founded in July of the same year. Perhaps this event finally

This wood-cut shows Alexander Graham Bell lecturing to an audience in Salem, Massachusetts. Through a telephone placed before his audience, the inventor communicated with his laboratory in Boston, fourteen miles away.

convinced the Hubbards that Alec could support their daughter. As part of his wedding present to her, Alec gave Mabel nearly all of his shares of stock in the Bell Telephone Company. On July 11, 1877, the couple was married at the Hubbard's house in Cambridge. At the time of their wedding, more than

200 telephones were in operation. In August, the number topped 700.

On August 4, seven years after his arrival in North America, Alexander Graham and Mabel Bell boarded a ship for England. They stayed in Europe for 15 months. During this time, Mabel gave birth to their first daughter, Elsie May Bell. Mabel said that Alec, like most new fathers, was "so fond of [Elsie] and yet so afraid of the poor little thing."

Without long hours of work and with his wife's good cooking, Alexander was growing stout. His worldwide reputation as an inventor was also growing. In January 1878, he received the command to demonstrate the telephone to Queen Victoria. The queen described the telephone as "most extraordinary." To Mabel, Bell described the queen as "humpy, stumpy, and dumpy."

Much was happening in the United States while Bell was away. Telephone wires had been strung among offices and homes across the country. Hubbard and Sanders were busy organizing business matters. In July, the Bell Telephone Company began to sell stock. But Western Union had started making and selling its own phones. President Orton claimed that his inventor, Elisha Gray, had the idea first. Watson told Bell that he was needed at home to defend the patent. Bell wrote, "Why should it matter to the world who invented the telephone so long as the world gets the benefit of it?" Still, he sailed home in October 1878. He was needed as a witness in court.

Western Union lost its battle with the Bell Company. But theirs was just the first of 600 lawsuits brought against Bell by jealous inventors and businessmen who wanted some of the telephone profits. The Bell Company won every case. And from his invention, Alexander Graham Bell became a millionaire.

Alexander Graham and Mabel Bell with their two daughters, Elsie May (left) and Daisy (front, center).

6

After the Telephone

Business owners soon began to see how useful telephones could be. People were proud to have telephones in their homes. In 1877, a telephone switchboard was put into service in Boston. The first telephone directory, just one page long, was published in New Haven, Connecticut. In the earliest days of the telephone, the person making the call had to push a knob before speaking. This made a thumping sound and got the attention of the person on the other end of the line. Soon the thump was replaced by a buzzer and later a bell. "Ahoy," the greeting that people first used, became "hello."

As the years passed, the telephone business became more complicated. Alexander Graham Bell let others make all the improvements. He was eager to move on to other projects. Bell wanted to prove his talents so that no one would think that he had "stumbled upon (one) invention and...there is no more good in me."

In the years after 1878, Bell invented an air conditioning system and a way to change seawater into drinking water. He experimented with X-ray devices and with sending speech and sounds over a beam of light. In the late 1800s and early 1900s, he tried sheep breeding. Bell wanted to find out if he could breed ewes that were more likely to have twins. Since most sheep have just one lamb at a time, ewes that were likely to have twins would be worth more money. He also made improvements on Thomas Edison's 1877 invention, the phonograph.

A family tragedy probably led to Bell's invention in 1881 of a "vacuum jacket." This medical machine was supposed to help people breathe. His newborn son had just died because of breathing problems.

Alexander Graham Bell (right) *watches while his grandchildren fly a kite he designed.*

The Bells lost another infant son two years later.

Other experiments had more pleasant roots. Since boyhood, Bell had been excited by flight. In the late 1880s and early 1890s, he dreamed of inventing a "flying machine." He also designed and flew kites, often with the help of eager grandchildren.

Bell's many inventions kept him quite busy in the years after his work on the telephone. But he seemed to bounce from one project to another. He had no focus, no firm goal. When he had worked on the telephone, he pushed himself hard, day after day for years. Never again did he approach a project with that same drive.

As a young man, Bell had been spurred on by the desire to do something great and to be worthy of the name of his well-known father. He also needed to make money so he could marry Mabel. Now he had done these things. As time passed, Bell's limited knowledge of science also caused problems. His career followed the pattern of many famous inventors: a single, great invention as a young man, followed by years of less important work.

Bell's many different interests certainly took time away from his scientific tasks. He gave time and money to the Montessori school movement and to magazines such as *Science* and *National Geographic.*

Whenever he could, he tried to improve the lives of deaf people. The Chicago and Cleveland public schools for the deaf that were named after him probably meant more to Bell than all the awards he received because of the telephone. He loved visiting deaf children, and they loved having him. During one visit to a deaf school, the children decided that this white-bearded, 250-pound man must be Santa Claus. They asked him how he was able to squeeze down chimneys. Bell made sure that George Sanders learned a trade and started his own business. He also offered support for his friend Helen Keller. In fact, his own daughters, Elsie May and Daisy, were a little jealous of all the time he spent with Helen. Strangely, the money Bell gave to the deaf community came from an invention that most deaf people would never use.

But in Bell's later life, he did not just work and lend support to needy people. He and Mabel enjoyed

their wealth, sometimes spending money before they got it. They traveled to England, France, Italy, Japan, and Mexico. The Bells held fancy parties. They had a huge house in Washington, D.C. But the summers there were too humid for Bell. To escape them, he had a mansion built in Nova Scotia, Canada, that he named "Beinn Bhreagh," which means "Beautiful Mountain." More than 30 people could stay there at one time. The Bells hired many servants to care for their guests and property. Over time, they added cottages, stables, a dairy, boathouses, a warehouse, and even a windmill. For 36 years, the Bells, their two daughters, and their many grandchildren spent happy summers on the house high on a hill overlooking the ocean. As a grandfather, Alexander especially enjoyed spending time with Elsie's young son Melville.

Although he never felt pressured by work, Bell kept his habit of working at night. Often he worked until three or four o'clock in the morning and then

Alexander Graham Bell with Helen Keller (left) and her teacher, Anne Sullivan.

slept until noon. Even as an old man, he preferred night to day, coolness to heat, and stormy, misty weather to bright sunshine.

Meanwhile, the telephone wires extended farther and farther west. They connected New York to Chicago and wooded villages to giant cities. Night and day across the country, the wires carried joyful news of births and marriages and graduations, and sad news of disappointments and deaths.

On January 25, 1915, Alexander Graham Bell was in New York, sitting at his desk near a telephone. Now 67 years old, he was called "Grampie" by his growing gang of grandchildren. Grandfather Bell had white hair and a white beard. In San Francisco, California, Thomas Watson waited to hear his friend's voice. The telephone company was preparing to connect the telephone lines from the east to the west coast. Company officials had arranged for these two men, the inventors of the telephone, to be the first to

As he grew older, Alexander Graham Bell enjoyed spending time with his grandchildren.

speak on this transcontinental telephone line.

"Mr. Watson, are you there?" Alexander Graham Bell asked.

"I hear you perfectly," Thomas Watson replied from across the continent.

In New York, the modern telephone equipment was replaced by a model of the Centennial telephone used in the early experiments. Bell picked up the old-fashioned instrument. It worked as well as the newer ones did.

"Mr. Watson," he said to his friend. "Come here—I want to see you."

Just before his 70th birthday, Alexander Graham Bell spoke to a group of young people. "It is a glorious thing to be old and look back upon the progress of the world during one's own lifetime...," he said. "I can remember the days when there were no telephones." When the inventor died on August 2, 1922, nearly 10 million telephones were in service. Today there are more than 425 million phones in use worldwide.

He was born with talent, patience, and determination. His interests were shaped by the Bells before him. Fate brought him to North America and Boston. In that American city he found the people and resources necessary for the invention of the telephone. Alexander Graham Bell will be remembered by most people as the inventor of our most popular and useful instrument of communication. But he would have wanted to be remembered first as a teacher of the deaf.

Index